The Elements of A

Putting pen to paper on a new page can be a little scary. How do you know that what you're doing will come out "right"? Happily, there is no right or wrong. There's just you, interacting with God's Word in whatever way pleases you. And it's easier than you think. All artists (whether they know it or not!) use some or all of the six elements below to express themselves. You can play with these elements to develop your own lettering and images.

Line

A line is any mark that spans a distance between two points. It can be straight or curved, thick or thin.

Shape

This is a closed line, or a defined area of space. It can be geometric like a square, free form like a blotch, or natural such as a tree or a body.

Space

Space is an area defined by the artist for a particular role, like the foreground or background. It is usually described as negative (the areas around other shapes) or positive (the areas within shapes.)

Texture

An easy way to think of this is that it's the visual equivalent of how something might feel, such as smooth, bumpy, rough, scaly, etc.

Form

An image has form if it has dimension, or volume. All real objects have form, but you can achieve the look of dimension with shading. So, a circle has shape but a drawing of a circle that's been shaded to look like a ball has shape and form.

Color

There are three properties to color: Hue, the name of the color such as yellow or blue; intensity, or how bright or dull the color is; and value, which describes how light or dark a color is.

Palettes

Color is one of the easiest and most evocative ways to express emotions, and it can be a comfortable way to get started journaling in your Bible. You can highlight words that have meaning to you in color, or start writing notes in the margin in colors that help you express how you feel as you meditate on the Scripture. As you get more comfortable, you can add colored imagery. Here are some color palettes that can help you express different moods:

Purples *Hope*

Reds *Joy*

Yellows *Optimism*

Blues *Tranquility*

Greens *Peace*

Grays *Struggle*

Pinks *Love*

Browns *Reflections*

The Promise of Bible Journaling

The Bible is God's expression of love to us, and it is bursting with His promises! I believe that God intended us to interact with the Bible, and Bible journaling is exactly that. Hebrews 4:12 describes the word of God as "living and active" and 1 Timothy 3:16 proclaims "all scripture is God-breathed." While you may indeed end up with a family keepsake, the treasure lies in your experience as you sit in the presence of God and meditate on and interpret His words, creatively with your own hands, guided by the Holy Spirit. It won't be long before you realize that Bible journaling is so much more than decorating your Bible.

One day while browsing Pinterest, I saw some Bible journal pages and immediately fell in love with the concept. While I relish an in-depth Bible study involving word studies, historical background, and theology, art journaling in my Bible is different. For me, it is all about worship. Drawing and painting have always been a huge part of my life. I have found my home in expressing my faith through the visual arts. However, there is just something a bit more personal when I journal directly in my Bible. In those quiet moments, it is just God and me.

On the practical side, you may be wondering where to begin or how to come up with ideas. I like to illustrate verses that speak directly to my current emotions or circumstances, or bring back sweet memories. For example, my grandmother was an organist in the church where my grandfather was the pastor. Recently I heard the hymn, "In the Garden," and was reminded of summers spent with my grandparents, and my mother's roses in her elaborate flowerbeds. A little research revealed that C. Austin Miles had been meditating on John 20 and awoke from a vision to write that hymn. Suddenly, my Bible needed some roses!

My technique is not elaborate. I approach my journaling Bible like a sketchbook. The drawing is my favorite part, and I especially love to "draw" words. I sketch lightly with a pencil, ink with a Micron pen, erase the pencil lines thoroughly, and then build up the color by layering with Prismacolor colored pencils. I like the simplicity. Let yourself be free to experiment and discover what works for you! There are so many tutorials and supplies available today to explore. Let them be inspiring, not intimidating. It is all about pursuing God. You will be overwhelmed at how easy He is to find.

I am thrilled to be able to share these designs with you here to help you begin to experience the joy and peace of Bible journaling. My deepest hope is that I can encourage you to open your Bible and connect with the Lord, whether for the very first time, or just the first time today.

—Krista Hamrick

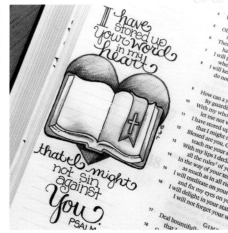

Above: One of my favorite techniques in Bible journaling is to incorporate words into my art, as I did with "Jesus" inside the heart. Pairing words and images helps me remember the text more easily.

Above: At first I was reluctant to draw over the text, but as I progressed I felt much more freedom to express myself.

Above: This is the last page of text in my Bible! I felt so much joy as I journaled this page.

Above: I found the Psalms to be one of the most accessible books to journal. The text is so inspiring, and the layout of the text on the page just seems to call out for art.

Above: Repeating a shape, such as these circular shapes, can be helpful in meditating on Scripture.

Above: Here's one of my favorite examples of combining bold art with a variety of different lettering.

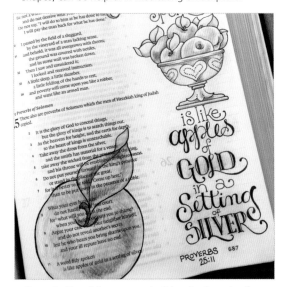

Above: Fruit and flowers, symbolizing the bounty of God's love, are consistent themes in my art.

Above: I also incorporate other themes, such as this patriotic one I created as I prayed for our country.

Above: Leaving white space surrounded by color, as I did with this dove, can really make an image stand out.

It is my prayer that your love may abound more and more

FOR TO ME

TO Live is CHRIST

and to die is gain.

PHILIPPIANS 1:21

1266

THE LETTER OF PAUL TO THE
PHILIPPIANS

Greeting

1 Paul and Timothy, servants[1] of Christ Jesus,

To all the saints in Christ Jesus who are at Philippi, with the overseers[2] and deacons:[3] [2] Grace to you and peace from God our Father and the Lord Jesus Christ.

Thanksgiving and Prayer

[3] I thank my God in all my remembrance of you, [4] always in every prayer of mine for you all making my prayer with joy, [5] because of your partnership in the gospel from the first day until now. [6] And I am sure of this, that he who began a good work in you will bring it to completion at the day of Jesus Christ. [7] It is right for me to feel this way about you all, because I hold you in my heart, for you are all partakers with me of grace,[4] both in my imprisonment and in the defense and confirmation of the gospel. [8] For God is my witness, how I yearn for you all with the affection of Christ Jesus. [9] And it is my prayer that your love may abound more and more, with knowledge and all discernment, [10] so that you may approve what is excellent, and so be pure and blameless for the day of Christ, [11] filled with the fruit of righteousness that comes through Jesus Christ, to the glory and praise of God.

The Advance of the Gospel

[12] I want you to know, brothers,[5] that what has happened to me has really served to advance the gospel, [13] so that it has become known throughout the whole imperial guard[6] and to all the rest that my imprisonment is for Christ. [14] And most of the brothers, having become confident in the Lord by my imprisonment, are much more bold to speak the word[7] without fear. [15] Some indeed preach Christ from envy and rivalry, but others from good will. [16] The latter do it out of love, knowing that I am put here for the defense of the gospel. [17] The former proclaim Christ out of selfish ambition, not sincerely but thinking to afflict me in my imprisonment. [18] What then? Only that in every way, whether in pretense or in truth, Christ is proclaimed, and in that I rejoice.

To Live Is Christ

Yes, and I will rejoice, [19] for I know that through your prayers and the help of the Spirit of Jesus Christ this will turn out for my deliverance, [20] as it is my eager expectation and hope that I will not be at all ashamed, but that with full courage now as always Christ will be honored in my body, whether by life or by death. [21] For to me to live is Christ, and to die is gain. [22] If I am to live in the flesh, that means fruitful labor for me. Yet which I shall choose I cannot tell. [23] I am hard pressed between the two. My desire is to depart and be with Christ, for that is far better. [24] But to remain in the flesh is more necessary on your account. [25] Convinced of this, I know that I will remain and continue with you all, for your progress and joy in the faith, [26] so that in me you may have ample cause to glory in Christ Jesus, because of my coming to you again.

[1] Or slaves (for the contextual rendering of the Greek word doulos, see Preface) [2] Or bishops; Greek episkopoi [3] Or servants, or ministers; Greek diakonoi [4] Or you all have fellowship with me in grace [5] Or brothers and sisters. The plural Greek word adelphoi (translated "brothers") refers to siblings in a family. In New Testament usage, depending on the context, adelphoi may refer either to men or to both men and women who are siblings (brothers and sisters) in God's family, the church; also verse 14 [6] Greek in the whole praetorium [7] Some manuscripts add of God

Above: I don't often use color over the entire page, but this is one example of a page where I simply felt inspired to use multiple bright colors. You don't have to stick to a single style!

Above: You don't have to use a lot of bright colors to create a beautiful page.

Above: I used a much darker, bolder text style here because I really wanted to concentrate on the words.

Above: On this page, I wanted to stay within the border, but I used color around certain words to highlight them.

Above: This page is an example of how I approach Bible journaling—as an extension of my everyday life.

If therefore the Son makes you free, YOU will be Free indeed.

JOHN 8:36

GROW

Be Still

Your Word is a L·A·M·P to my feet and a light for my Path

PSALM 119:105

We are blessed with PEACE

PSALM 29:11

Holy Spirit

He tells me I am His Own

In the Garden c. Austin Miles

be transformed by the r·e·n·e·w·a·l of your mind

ROMANS 12:2

For I know that my Redeemer lives!

JOB 19:25

I do set my rainbow in the cloud,

GENESIS 9:13

And it shall be for a token of a covenant between me and the earth

PEACE

Freedom in Christ

Grace through Faith

EPHESIANS 2:8

JOY

DEUTERONOMY 7:9

HIS LOVE never fails

I was glad when they said unto me Let us GO into the House of the LORD

PSALM 122:1

how long, o Lord?

But I have trusted in thy mercy: my heart shall rejoice in thy salvation. I will sing unto the Lord, because He hath dealt bountifully with me.

Psalm 13:5,6

I will lift up my eyes to the HILLS. where does my help COME FROM? My help comes from the Lord who made Heaven and EARTH.

PSALM 121:1,2

I am redeemed

Truth

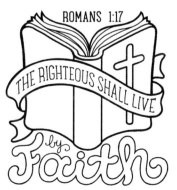

ROMANS 1:17

THE RIGHTEOUS SHALL LIVE by Faith

I have loved You with an Everlasting Love

JEREMIAH 31:3

Step out in faith

Amazing Grace How Sweet the sound

Heaven

Power

amen

Earth

A B C D E F G
H I J K L M N
O P Q R S T ?
U V W X Y Z !
a b c d e f g h i j
k l m n o p q r
s t u v w x y z

Give us this day our daily bread.

And forgive us our debts, as we forgive our debtors.

And lead us not into temptation but deliver us from evil.

For thine is the Kingdom and the Power and the Glory FOREVER

Matthew 6:9-13

amen

I have called YOU by name, YOU ARE Mine

ISAIAH 43:1

Our Father which art in Heaven, Hallowed be thy name. thy Kingdom come. Thy will be done on Earth as it is in Heaven.

LORD, help me GROW according to Your Word

FOR TO ME

To Live is CHRiST

He who began a Good work in you will complete it until the day of Jesus Christ

PHILIPPIANS 1:6, 21

Alleluia

the FRUIT of the SPIRIT is LOVE JOY PEACE Patience Kindness GOODNESS Faith Gentleness and SELF-CONTROL

Galatians 5: 22,23

Hallelujah

Jesus is born!

LUKE 2:7

I will sing unto the Lord, because He hath dealt bountifully with me.

Celebrate Him

Seek Him

Rejoice

PSALM 13:5

Matthew

Mark

I HAVE HIDDEN
Your Word
in
my heart

Luke

John